COME

BY THE SAME AUTHOR

POETRY

Wao

Fab

Boo!

tink

Think?

Bugalugs

tree

until

HOODOO

OPEN

Autumn

COME

by

PAUL BLOUNT

THE CLUNY PRESS
ST. ASAPH
2023

First published in 2023 by

The Cluny Press
Eirianfa
The Roe
St. Asaph
Denbighshire
LL17 OLU
Wales

A CIP catalogue record for this book is available from the British Library

ISBN 978-1-8383950-2-5

Designed and typeset by Discript Limited, Chichester
Printed in England by TJ Books, Padstow

To see a world in a grain of sand
And a heaven in a wild flower,
Hold infinity in the palm of your hand
And eternity in an hour.

William Blake, *Auguries of Innocence*

For

Sophia

Contents

I

II

III

IV

V

I

Camille Pissarro

From St. Thomas a virgin boy in a Virgin Isle,
the first Jew to crush lapis lazuli from Afghanistan
into an evanescent style.
From Paris in spooky streets
where the hunchback of Notre Dame shrieked
his nascent cry and rang his tolling bell
in quiet landscapes filled with girlie Lorettes,
Pissarro met Monet from Le Havre
and the two plotted their escape from hell.
A small town Jewish boy broke the Hebrew law
and taught the stones to draw.

Hilaire-Germain-Edgar Degas

A draughtsman at heart, ungovernable
in black and white.
A banker's bourgeois son who loved Longchamp
and the gee-gees, contorted prostitutes
and actresses in pastel pinks and horse groom brown,
floaty fogs of blue ballet rats.
The everyday dancers with the clown.

My mother, riven, croaked in a pastel sheen,
her lungs in a river muddied by a faulty gene,
I, at her bedside asked if she liked Degas.
She said 'No, Shelley, and to give up
the divine nature of light.'
Let god croak.
That immense yellow disc withdrawn
from my mother that night,
and I closed her eyes to keep Shelley in,
and Degas out.
But I liked Degas: every day when
I went to visit Grandma I had love
and every day I returned I did not.

Paul Cézanne

Cézanne went with Émile Zola to scrump
for apples in Manet's orchard,
an innocent rich boy who could afford
to be an artist in brothels carved out of tar,
dark brown brothels with women from the street
with no money to feed their families.
Coarse, in outdoor colour, where life stops still
an unreserved romantic with a predilection
for rough sex. Then a pupil of Pissarro
he wished to be Poussin and gain nature again
in which the apples were plastic, his art
an elastic band.

Claude Monet

With brushwork as quick as kids
running toward the sea on a sunny day,
Monet painted the colour of time,
from his room at the Savoy
where, in Thames and Parliament mist,
he painted on the chocolate box a rhyme
which kept him from the Lorettes' pox.

Painting *en plein air* using an app.

Claude followed another Claude
with a different take on water and light,
and pieced together a jigsaw of a different map,
to leave Van Gogh his starry night.

Pierre Auguste Renoir

Pink flamingos dress the wallpaper,
not a William Morris design.
It gave the secret away.
Not quite chocolate box, but very French woke,
combined with surround sound.

When I awoke and found woke
plastered on the front pages,
I thought of Renoir, the facile,
the decorative Boucher's colouring.
With Monet and Bazille in Barbizon,
you alone paint beautiful scenes,
lovely women, children and flowers.
No black Van Gogh, where miss,
with her skirt pulled down,
wearing such a frown
in a rainbow meadow by the Seine,
the ancient sacred pretty river,
painted by Renoir in a quiet shiver,
against a background of no sound.

Frédéric Bazille

The requirement was for cohesive behaviour.
The Anglo-Saxons filed in to vote
by the snake-oil salesman's placards
to catch a moment of saviour.
Bazille and Monet went to Honfleur
to paint out of doors, in the open air
and carry his fleur-de-lis on top
of his battle axe, the royal arms of France
displayed in painted mute tones
but a German bullet left him with no chance
to show a wolf moon in night light.

Berthe Morisot

No black for Miss Little Goody Two Shoes,
passed from Corot to Manet to Renoir.
The poster girl worked in white brush strokes.
She be a wild she, she be, black eyed
and fancy free, opening in fifths
as the monks had once done
and their chant a force in a grandad's clock,
when I thought you had gone wearing red shoes
striking the Notre Dame chime, always a peacock.

Mary Cassatt

A spooky Yank from far away
with a faraway Degas gaze
and a skirt swirl like a whirling dervish
in flavours of the Levant in an American phrase,
not heard by Hezbollah practising ikebana.
Looking at pink in pink glasses
to harmonise and smear the colour in the zenana
absorbed in Virginia Woolf white
to be drowned in the muddy river Ouse.
Wearing white Japanese petticoats in lace
with an incompetent cervix,
painted mothers and children to hide her face,
in Prussian blue paint and Japanese graphics.

Gustave Caillebotte

Another stinking rich kid with time for art,
who sought a firebreak between
the Spring-Judas tree and opulence;
a discontinuity and de-emphasis on structure,
a lack of permanence.

An artist of incidents rather than the all-embrace:
Cold War grey face.
A nuclear submarine left in the dark
to dawdle.

Paul Gauguin

Like Ibsen he seemed to live in an attic
with no light.
The creole mole who danced to no one's jig
in brothels painted in coal, cool to the touch,
nudes with no soul, so infra dig.
The stockbroker's selection of a girl
to stand in a sewage channel in an Afghan,
looking at a floral display squeezed out of a twirl,
with cold eyes to perform a can-can.

In the charcoal black mine
he ate a luscious furry peach
and tasted the colour peach black,
which made the repressed bohemian overreach
to seek the *fin de siècle* primitive.
Went native in Tahiti, the symbolic patterns
and linear rhythms of nature he sought,
to paint in sensuous disport.

Vincent van Gogh

One day a frog jumped from a lily pad
into Monet's pond and came out with ginger hair
and a mirror for self-examination.
He painted in milky green absinthe
and drank his paint,
and looked at himself for self-humiliation.
The frog hopped into the coal mine
forgetting there was not a pond covered in a lily pad
but potato fields in peasant dirt with swine.
Rejected a *smörgåsbord* of styles, no cherubs there
for brush-strokes gone mad in aesthetic pain.

The frog kept inflatable rubber dolls,
looking rather bored, in a corner of his room.
But they are not all that remain.
Eight hundred paintings
and eight hundred and fifty drawings,
a reminder to the insane.

Georges Seurat

A strange stiffness in pink dots.
A rich boy painting working-class boys
on the Left Bank of the Seine.
Blue, red and green colour into white light
in the after-image with too many dots
making the insane.

Journeys to the sea, to the north,
watery sticks with licks of pigment.
Can-can dancers to the south,
at the circus, gaiety stiff in bourgeois decay
in *peinture optique.*
His pointillist technique as pointless
as a frost in May.

II

William Blake

A loner, largely unloved and ignored
who saw angels in a tree on Peckham Rye,
and forced us to ask the question why?

He drew a gothic living form
in a tree, a flowering line which drew
Jesus, as imagination, asleep and awake
and within ourselves at each daybreak.
Everything in the tree was holy and divine,
to reveal the divinity within ourselves.

William Blake did Newton hate,
his measurement of Cotgrove's science allowed
to poison the tree
and loose the hold on the real world,
but what is reality?
When playing hoopla with the angels
he drew the golden string of infinity
and lost his virginity gently in a Jerusalem tree.

William Wordsworth

Darkness with the light of snow,
the fleeting nature of hope,
yellow daffodils circled by a black crow,
a man wearing a long cloak in taupe
with a sister on his arm and Coleridge
walking alongside spouting about his knowledge
and thinking if Dorothy was ginger
downstairs, Coleridge liked ginger with his dope.
Another rich boy with time on his hands
to play a part in others' art,
circled by a black crow, Coleridge with his beau.

Samuel Taylor Coleridge

It probably all began wrong, the bipolar,
married life a wreck, nightmares a wreck,
illnesses a wreck, opium addiction a wreck.
Two quarts of laudanum a week laced with Coca-Cola,
listening to 'Rime of the Ancient Mariner'
by the heavy metal band Iron Maiden,
in a rolling swell of turgid constipation.
The forever sinner with Marxist redden
on his blush face for hiding secret knowledge,
gained through disgrace at Wordsworth's hands,
suspended in disbelief.

A will-o'-the-wisp utopian through opium
sought to change the world in delirium
and ecstatic vision.
On it, drinking the milk of paradise.
Under its influence all made sense,
making an ugly place better.
Like Schubert's hurdy-gurdy man
his plate was always empty.

Thomas De Quincey

He confessed to taking twelve thousand
drops of laudanum a day;
enough to kill a horse.
The opiate gave a sensual effect
on his unconscious mind.
When trips went bad he felt the force
as the traumas rattled his cage into a rage
against humanity and Freud's talking cure.

On Saturday nights, fish and chip specials
with opium salted on to keep the poor
warm and quince fruit tarts
with lemon drizzle opium cake
washed down with Quincy from the upper Loire.

The river he did not understand
as it entered the sea. So he pushed
and pushed and pushed until he felt free.

A right wing neo-Nazi,
who believed in aristocratic privilege
and salted his knowledge in sacrilege
in a pocket full of loose change.

Lord Byron

The Harrow boy, a bisexual letch
who became a right honourable wretch
with a dad called 'Mad Jack'
who also raked his seed, his first reflex.
Byron jnr. another romantic addict,
this time for sex, with your wife, daughter
or anyone's ex.

How great your power, m'lord
to shag the maid servant in the dark
and leave her in the family way
to earn no pennies to keep her family,
dismissed as a used, covered filly in your park.
An echo of another Lord with seventy-seven wifelets
acquired to show his power and size of his assets.

In Greece the rich boy had found his cause:
Greek emancipation from the Ottoman,
appearing as the hero from Nietzsche's
übermensch, or superman,
meanwhile the sodomite garnered boys.

At Cambridge University he kept a tame bear
and proposed it for a fellowship
to accord with his Lordship.
Lady Caroline Lamb claimed Byron was
'mad, bad and dangerous to know.'

After smeared incest with his half-sister,
she had a child.
It was said he could write some useful stuff
if not a touch wild,

when he could take his face out of his
maid servants' muff.

Not just a foot deformed, but the man,
like a self-promoting rock DJ,
the Jimmy Savile of his day.

He was such a literary rock star
that in death the British Museum,
St. Paul's Cathedral, the National Gallery
and Westminster Abbey
wanted nothing to do with him or his la-di-da.
But now, sanitised, the paedophile
reinvented with new stripes
is lamented and considered tactile.

Percy Bysshe Shelley

It must have been a beautiful country
when the buffaloes ran wild:
this is England in Arcadia.
When the cockerel could crow cock-a-doodle-do
it needed Sid Vicious to go nuclear,
slaughter the buffaloes
and bring in an aristo-punk, son of a baronet toff,
bad boy, a cowboy with two guns.
Enter Percy Bysshe Shelley.
Bang, bang you're dead England.

Constantly under the gaze of MI6 and MI5
the itinerant went into a skydive
knocking off women, having kids
in a punk-rock Mohican hippie style.
His groupies crowded into communes
later formed by Lenin and his tycoons.

He sought the buffaloes in ghost ponds
but found English bigwigs were in pig
and waved their magic wands
to summon the match girls from the wild west
to show their breasts on page three,
the *Daily Telegraph* readership could not believe:
Catholic emancipation, atheism, free-love, vegetarianism,
the political radical who described humanitarianism.

At Petersfield the tempo changed, the in pig
delivered and Shelley scribbled non-violent resistance.
The young punk rocker sang in rage,
to the plight of the Red Indian now the buffaloes had gone.

He saw a girl walking through a gale
with wild swans about her swirl
and took her for his love with a gift
of mother-of-pearl. He wrote in a buzz
of static charge as the Petersfield militia charged,
bayonets and sabres unshielded
to cut the dormouse in the field in two.
The world untrue.

The poster boy of the avant-garde;
the Mick Jagger of his age
who ended up a wise sage,
talking to Blake's angels who were in flight,
frit of the pack in attack.
A can-do guy who did not leave
upon a quiet conscience. But voted Green
and said it with no nonsense.

The bad juju darkness left
as he went to his better angels,
in silk balloons into the starlit night
carrying his political message a declaration of rights.

John Keats

Difficult stuff, classical allusions.
Highbrow, a thinker; a big thinker
ironing out confusions.
High Corinthian ideals
contained in a serious mind.
No drugs, no sex, no rock and roll
just a wanting to be kind
to words written in darkness,
disease and depression.
Waiting for his last hour
as in the first World War
Wilfred Owen laid down his premature fate.

Little of loving, of dance: cerebral
made from Colosseum stone to form a white face
showing no trace of marble lines,
too young to grow. Perhaps too deep
for English taste, a sensuality
not given to our sentimentality.
The truth of the imagination being beauty
is languorously narcotic,
so wise.
God pronounced him dead at twenty-five.

III

The Demographic Of My Complaint

The demographic of my complaint
goes back to Ancient Greece
and the theory of democracy,
born when roses grew wild
and the red kites flew low
over the new-mown grass,
mowed low.

The hill fort creaked in the wind,
made from mud, wood and the theory of oligarchy;
louche.
Built with Greek Ionic stone pretence
by a stage performer wearing greasepaint,
who formed a bent muddied cartouche.
He launched low, fast missiles aimed at
children's eyes,
in the Ukraine for political gain:
his hill fort sacrificial burial ground,
with ravens cack-cacking above the ground.
His people wanted to vote for a nice Stalin,
but found that human rights are an illusion
in a mug shot of disillusion.

Fintry, August Morning Sky

Rapidly the wind changed to still
the morning sky,
underdown Mallard feathered morning sky.
Country hill streaks of an abstract painting:
modernism against early pre-dawn full moon,
lit light blue: no background back sky,
and further back stars,
and further back
the still chaos of closed knowledge.

I thought you a daisy kind of person,
but in the night I thought you would destroy me
like a china doll,
smashed according to your aesthetic protocol.

Kyiv

A monster is drawn by small children
in scrap-books in pen and ink tied with a red ribbon
or in water-colours with fangs
in dreams wet in the bed listening to bangs
for fear in the night where, with no light,
they cannot see him coming near,
the bogeyman,
the nice Stalin, as he was called,
Mr Putin who replaced the clergyman.
Red carpet ready to make a splash,
by a smash of small children's dreams
while hiding his cash with his gang of thieves.

The small children's monster is now in
the Hall of Fame; Hitler, Stalin, Putin
and his name will remain
for mothers to come to tell their young
of the monster who could dream
of total death as part of his deranged scheme.

The Wind Through The Trees

The wind through the trees sounded like the sea,
the eastern Mediterranean sea,
or through Lebanon pines and succulent vines,
or the aspen tink, fluttering pink.

Comic strips for children will cost you a lot,
the nits in their hair, the filthy louse in the thirties
school inspection.
What dress size did women wear in the dark ages?
When men climbed all over them de-lousing
their hair and seeding their spores and called
them their little wee pet.
The women kept going like the Duracell bunny
until the batteries ran out,
and the coffee smell created a different persona.

Be a non-Teflon woman, stick to it
my little wee pet
and have lots of fun being dead:
nothing any more to worry about, no more
wind through the trees sounding like the sea.

There's Not Too Much Savouring The Meal

There's not too much savouring the meal
with a Komodo dragon, no prissiness.
Why do we test ourselves under time?
Explosion of thought. Karl Marx. Ukraine.
No grain, no gain.
I lost my ring in a strong swell,
she was an old gold ring, pretty,
my second ring down a deep well
and I thought what god did accord
to the daily grind of the stone age stone
on the quern, grinding the corn.
Don't take the fern. Get out. Explosion.
Quick, run. But I've got my exam on Tuesday.
Get out. Run.
But what is this Vladimir Putin doing?
I've got my exam on Tuesday.

Shortest Day

On this the shortest day, chasing the light
looking for the poster boy of the insect world,
a bumble bee in fresh new light,
long tongued they tell no lies
and are clean with pollen soaked heads
as Grandma said cleanliness is next
to godliness.

I searched and found my bumble bee,
but she were not what she appeared to be.
She be a wild bee, with
a short tongue, and she led me
a merry dance on the shortest day,
and lied.

When You Came To Ukraine

On Midsummer's day when the raptors circled,
you first came to cut the lavender
in the field, to starve the bumble bee;
the honey from the bee,
and the raptors with the woodlander could see.

On the second time you came
to cut the lavender in the field,
you made sure in the evening the woodlander
could not wash the baby in the sink.
There was no sink.
There was no baby;
just cut lavender flattened pink.

The Farmer Had Left The Field Fallow

The farmer had left the field fallow
for a year, then the cows came,
then the crows, or I thought them crows
but jackdaws they be, a mass of black
jackdaw crows buzzing *Kaarr.* Jumping Jack Flash
it was a gas, seeing the mass circle high.
Strutting their stuff.
Kaarr, Karen you black witch, watch
the flight of the clatter of the train,
claw your way away from me,
Kaarr, Karen I'll never see your mass again.
Away black witch to where you came
and circle your kraal as you fly to Yell.

Ukraine Orchard

Prove it.
Someone grew those trees in numbers.
Logic is the hygiene, cleansing.
Bach invented new numbers,
negatives and the imaginaries, in the *Well-Tempered Clavier.*

What do we mean by I define oneness? Proof.
Irrational numbers. What do we mean by 3?
The different noises made by nightjars
in the orchard. Pythagoras and his whole numbers
did not see the orchard clean.

The most famous irrational number is π,
but in the orchard there is no pattern:
the decimal places go on forever.

For the Hindus zero was a number in its own right.
Nothingness in the orchard was accorded its abstract value.
Division by zero is infinity.
It is proven in the orchard by the apple tree,
by the queen bee,
who murders her kind with a dreadful unkind.

The Pigs Went Wild

The pigs went wild on the day
their throats were due to be cut;
escaped their pen.
Some went to the moon wood,
others elsewhere, to the pear wood.
Those in the pear wood were captured
but those in the moon wood were not
and went wild, feral from innocence
to experience and forever smiled.

Burying The Dead

With Walt Whitman and his box
of lost thoughts, there weren't very many
to bury, the lambs they were difficult that year.
The perfume masked the smell of the
tannery and the rot,
giving off the sweetest sound,
the sweetest sound of all.
It was the time of year when
the wind stopped at the blind oak tree.
For crying out loud, forget to concentrate
on the sacred, the land of the
summer people, carib coloured
when Plato thought what love was
in a Greek wonderland fast asleep,
mathematically bent,
its rhythmic chant demanding love
in this time of Lent.
The resonance had been where the lambs
were born, across from the field of corn,
the killing field. We tossed them in the
glacial lake hoofed to the farm.
As Tolstoy said we get glimpses of happiness.

Let Us Play With Form

Let us play with form, here is your stick,
I have mine.
The pink horse did not like the snow,
nor its rider and they froze to death
by the beck, like Tinkerbell
who nipped like a crow and grew and grew
into loud.
So in the shadows and doubts of the night
you reappeared with your light
and the snowdrops came again.

You showed me hopscotch, calligraphy
and the little tap of the fingernail
against the vein.

The calligraphy on the cave wall
showed the pink horse, the hopscotch
and the little tap of the fingernail
against the vein,
which made the pink horse pass the fast fire
of harsh and frenzied colour
in uniform neglect.

Victory Day Parade, Red Square

A small trill in half-sunlight,
the Dark Ages come to new light.
Transmutability, from gold to old.
Beaker people came later, before Putin.
Later, after Spong Man and the cry of tin,
as fragile as Terry's Chocolate Orange,
liquid fire to metal sword,
the cutting edge intercontinental ballistic missile
greeted by Putin with a wry smile.
Ten warheads reference *The Scream.*

With mezzotint tonal variation
they had a Z on their tanks in Ukraine,
to imprint their silly boat, taken out from the moat
of racial purity.
When the top does not hear the bottom
there is a crack in the beaker pot
and the fabric comes apart at the seams.

Wigmore Hall

Whenever I enter this space
I feel I am entering a cocoon of class,
as when my grandmother would hug me
and I smelt her rosemary by the sunglass.

Bad light had stopped play in the lockdown year.
Bloch had a prayer for cello and piano near
and in Wigmore Hall, the two figures
played between the flowers for us all,
and I smelt her rosemary.

Punk Thatcherites

Punk Thatcherites paint the sheep pink
and present them as an art installation,
silvered with hot lime and heavy damask rosewater
and spray neonicotinoids, banned for bees,
a blueprint for Putin's horror in Ukraine.

A naturally dyed blue Tory wearing the skein
would wish a Medieval knight to reappear
and remind the world of chivalry, courtly manners
and courtly love when on Crusade we obeyed
and never stepped outside the Code.
As Thatcher never stepped outside the code
on sinking the Belgrano to save her glow.

IV

Komitas

Tip, skip, flip, lisp your lines
Komitas lend me your skipping rope
in the low lying grassy plain
shell blown by the wind.

Listen to the rustle of the low grass,
in the machir, as the woodman
cut the wood into a bodge,
a different grown wood for the Samhuinn,
when the fire would mean endlessness.
New frog, I place its Celtic slime against your forehead, kiss you,
and place the frog gently, into the pond;
flop, flip, lisp your lines.

Komitas' Armenian Tunes

The autumn sun splayed through the window,
Komitas' Armenian tunes came early
this autumn afternoon, *Seven Folk Dances.*
When warmth was drawn from the ice cube
at the point.
To bring us to the point: the Ukraine.
Why did you close the window from the autumn sun?
Is it to keep us sane
from the ghosts that flood in their sound?
And scrap for food not allowed
on each note sound
and fear an early bed or an early dead
carrying the seed into the memory.

Imbolc: 30 January

Spring was starting to stir in the belly
of Mother Earth.
Pagan fire nettle and wood mixed with man's desire
produced a Machiavelli to haunt a human mind.
Tension in the form of a spring
about to be sprung. The new creation
of the young, a pickle in the gritty
soft soil,
chivalry and perfect nights.

With increasing light and increasing heat
the free spirit released harum-scarum
and the pagan wrote *The Rite of Spring*
and the pagan squirted his seed
into the woman
and when her belly was full he felt
his duty done to Mother Earth
and the ways of his day.

Messiaen Catalogue d'Oiseaux

I pay only cash for ethics and morals
when the dinosaurs existed.
Tip your trash into someone else's garbage can.
There are no scraps in my scrap-book.
And why do we need them now, the dinosaurs,
more trash, more cash?
You remember E.coli? We now got covid,
salmonella, flu, pox.
You got pox in some psychedelic hinterland
in an oblique way, *amour fou,* as the French say.

Crash the keys, be the big man you little squirt,
be a soprano in the church.
Let's hear your voice sing, not *das unheimliche*
uncanny or weird, but treble with the bird
pecking at toadflax and the leech.

I have known some silly girls, glitter girls,
sparky, red, blonde, things in pink.
I have known some serious girls
in the divinity of signatures
who could cut off a glowing finger for the ring
and pocket it as trash, strapped for cash.

In an odyssey penned by Homer,
omnipresence is a dark place
wherein an apple tree orchard with piglets
and truffles record in a black book
where Merlin was entombed.
Merlin the magician whose magic never
fooled the crash of morals chasing cash,
to the sound of the song thrush in the
apple tree.

Cleansing Out With Messiaen

Cleansing out with Messiaen,
colourless, cold and less
made Machiavelli look
like a social worker
seeded in a scared sward,
she was colour-blind you see.

She made great hoofs of sound
pussyfooting around, blind chemistry
until Christmas
then, every so often the mob
is restructured; the dead wood
cleared out, like a crucifixion.
A cleansing.
In a bubble-gum pink brogue
no longer in vogue.

She Kept Her Secrets

She kept her secrets in small sachets,
which Schoenberg opened one by one
at night, she asleep, her purse
coloured Prussian blue concealed
the sachets' scented hue.

Twelve sachets he unveiled
as he touched her shoulder to awake
a song cycle, the top of her shoulder bare.
The rubato was in tempo. Freedom with order,
resolving with a cadence on the tonic in D minor.

In the olden days, the Romano-British days,
before the Vindaloo or a good pint before midnight
or Schoenberg's shame when your name
came floating along
and the snapdragon snapped you up
I touched your shoulder as he had done
and with a glass of sparkling water tinged
as you lit the stage.

Joy And Her Blackcap Bird

She sang in the church choir,
she sang a Gregorian chant,
with high notes held, until she was felled.
After the felled in the late winter she asked
'Have I seen a Blackcap in my garden world?
Call a hard tak, song a rambling chattering,
as if after chemo and radio,
but each phrase ending with a crescendo of beauty.'
I held her back but her black caught her late,
and came back again.

Mahler 2, Proms

Mahler 2, Proms.
Brass, bash, slash; rash of notes
sounds like a pigman's cottage,
beloved by Simon Rattle.
So we have to suffer this prattle
'cause the prat was knighted,
now sainted by the establishment
as a form of punishment.

Mahler, a Jew who converted to Christianity
to save his soul and career,
writing about the Resurrection.
A traitor proclaimed by a similar
on hearing a mass of French irony
before the final dance in ebony.

If you emulate something
someone has already done,
you are not yourself,
so who is your self?
But a cartouche
remained trapped in flint-lined amber.

V

The Girls Waddled, As Girls Do

The girls waddled, as girls do
with thick hips and big tits
to *Primark* stores with no thoughts
as three thousand years ago
they waddled through the bracken, oats and rye.

Mummy made me a black box
and put me inside so I couldn't see,
but I pricked a hole through and saw
the other bits of the girls with no thoughts.

When mummy let me out I met a girl
who shopped with no thought
and asked why she was such a tart
to shop at *Primark*.

She said she couldn't give a fuck about poverty,
about exploitation and cheap labour
in some foreign dump.
She cared about a black bloke performing Grime
in a bulletproof vest with a Union Jack flag
at Glastonbury
and the aesthetic of the sublime.

University Days

A parable is a fine thing
when looking for a university town,
to achieve great things and wear the gown.
So I came to Bath to see if there was bullshit
behind the neo-classical façade
and found Cotgrove who laughed out loud
about the idea of freedom of thought.

A conchy from WW2 with a yellow streak
and a fascist's hatred for open-speak
who taught nought.
But as an eighteen-year-old boy I was too stupid not to spot
a fanatic Nazi in a banker's gown.
So I chose to walk on a glacier
and enjoy white water rafting in its white ice melt
away from the words of a bigot financier
who fancied his own bullshit hidden behind a façade.

A parable is a fine thing, but a saying in which something
is expressed in terms of something else
can end as a yellow streak.
He scoffed at flying kites on moonlit nights
and thoughts outside the cell.
A university man alright,
tightened around his ideological fright.

Before God

Before god, finding the light,
bold treatment of low tones,
of black holes and artistry
were crucified along the Appian Way.

I awoke to woke on Radio 4.
We got a Chinese virus,
and will end with a Chinese society.
The Church of England is Shinto,
primitive Christianity, linked to monarchy.
Before god, the virus finding the light,
learned to tread with bold treatment
of low tones.

Your Skin Shone Like Heather

Your skin shone like heather brushed with frost
as we walked with no talk
looking for purity
and stumbled on snowdrops, or Candlemass bells,
in the ditch where the church now lives.

We passed a fold of red cattle
with uncouth highland horns
which could pierce purity with woke,
spoke on a broken wheel.
From the clerestory we saw the deil*
and watched his ways with woke iconoclasm
as he excised the snowdrops in the ditch.

---

* deil: Scots for devil

Ēostre

Ēostre, an Anglo Saxon goddess,
borrowed the idea from Eve;
the idea of the forbidden bite,
with a pet hare at her feet,
Ēostre arranged her set as god would have done.

The maids were lined up one by one
above the hill, under an ancient oak tree
and given chocolate eggs to be rolled down
to waiting thanes, expectant.
Inside the eggs was oestrogen cream
and when the winning maid would bite
she would conceive.

At Christ's resurrection the race was held
and the maid Mary won the race,
dressed in hot pink gauze, à la mode.
Under the ancient oak Mary bit through
the chocolate egg into the oestrogen cream,
but a bough of the tree was hazardous
and, as she bit, snapped clean.

And Easter day was born,
and Ēostre's pet hare was seen no more.

Sturgeon

I thought I had seen everything with Thatcher,
then came Sturgeon: I thought it was
a Russian fish, not a Stalinist dish,
or milk-snatcher.
She plays with rubato but the pulse
does not change, as in an unfinished Delacroix,
a cacophony in G Minor,
a flat bottomed stack barge with a red gaffed
sheet sail and wonky eyeliner.
She pouts pretentious rant,
like an Orwellian rat caught in her own trap,
as the nodding dogs clap
and the demagogue smears Scottish political clap.

In The Strawberry Fields

In the strawberry fields
with nobody's jig and sweet notes
with Shelly and joggings at end
Jigs were three pence a nod, if
she could last that long
guzzling on strawberries
and that sort in the field,
if she could last that long.

But what of he?
He, the man he wanted to be
how long would he last in his
love in the strawberry field
when sour fruit proves him wrong
and her quite right that straw dried night?

In Fruity Farm

In fruity farm where the raspberries grew,
and the goosegogs blew wild, spiky, abrasive,
are you still the silly buzzy bee I relive
hanging by the tree coming home to me?
With yellow stripes and funky chop-chop spikes
and a memento for all times sake,
of deep time into the black
where the pigs squeal when we slit their throats at night.
But we meant no harm, just made a living
and you in your bright blue dress
came down the stairs and talked of forgiving
the Muslim with muslin across your face.

The Man Went First To Pick The Tangerines

The man went first to pick the tangerines.
The woman went second, dressed in aquamarine
in the Orange Free State.

The hill fort was in a beech wood,
not my favourite tree, too cold
in December snow, the under too sterile
the bark too tactile, like your skin
in the cold.
Like the alchemists of old
who turned the rhythm of life to gold,
you were bound by nothing.
When we went to Tangier
tied together in each other's fear.

I came out first with the tangerine,
you, I lost in the tangerine field filled with fear.

Clear

It's clear,
if you don't have a history
what do you have?
We are governed by the wind, the sea
and the land,
the colour of green in the rocks.
The Protestants ransacked my home,
which had stuck together for many years.
We live in the remains,
the Protestants' gains.
We listen to the sea and the skylark
watching Teuchars sunbathing on the beach
drinking clear Luksusowa potato vodka martini
listening to Puccini
and Mercator's squaring of the circle.
It's all there in the seed head, underneath
a black Russian funny fur hat
over the clear corpse.

Death Of A Prime Minister's Mother

Sleeping on the streets, still life
in December snow, cold light
wrapped in a newspaper cutting
of a prime minister's mother no longer alive,
a painter it said, often naïve,
with a debt to the Fauvists, or maybe
a Vorticist with inspired fantasy cityscapes.

Sleeping on the streets in December snow
you know a fantasist when he shows
to exalt pure colour,
in his fat blue eyes you see countless
lies, as his mother painted bad pictures.
He inherited her genes:
a cityscape with the next warm colour to glow.
Think of the Eton boy who whines
in hyperbolic lies sleeping on the streets
in December snow.

Above My Home

Above my home lies an iron age fort
in which women gave birth
with iron age clamps
in a cold December wind or storm.

I know this through the new religions
and I look through a god shaped hole
described by a senior lecturer in Sociology
and Social Policy, wearing pink.
So let's deconstruct the shindig
and sociological pompoms
and keep clipping the coupons
for a lottery heyday.

Manchester

Do wear your cool white vest
against your Afro shirt
as you explain you are not just another name,
like Alexander the Great,
with an oriental theory based in Greek dark matter,
and ox-eye daisies, the chatter of the blind
June birds in summer song,
which proved you wrong.

I want reparations, man, now
from you, a white slaver who done me wrong,
or a black tyre to sling round your white waist
and ignite to burn retribution into
the redistribution from the slave.

Forget William Cobbett's *Rural Rides*
and his Manchester factories piled high with cotton fluff:
working class starving in squalor and lung dust.
It's Black Lives Matter.
Forget your Manchester slums, your
skinny kids and mums with skinny breasts
they're just white.

Fog in Japan

Baby boy made quite a big splash
making fog in Japan.
The atom man sipping black tea with the
orang-utan, happy-go-lucky with finesse
flicked the switch and could not care less
as he tightened the Celtic torque
around loose talk of loss of the
orang-utan.
Lost in the fog, baby boy made in Japan
when the carnival ended the last dance
which no one could see through,
then we used napalm in Vietnam.
The cherry blossom trees could not be
seen, or touched, only smelt, and the acrid smell
of the orang-utan singing in melt.

I Know You Are Both Dead

I know you are both dead
but I am not going to allow
you to talk to me the way
you do any more.
Splish, splash memories,
day and night.
I am not going to clean your
dirty kitchen floor
that you dirty more now you're dead.
I did stay with one of you in
your deathbed, the other not
because to me you were forgot.
Do not talk to me the way
you do any more.

Cairn

The stone lain was lain again and again,
the next stone lain was lain and lain again.

Closed, the killed were laid to create
a different god. Fearful, in Evensong.

Spinoza

There's always marriage as an option
before the little bird lands in the tumble dryer
and the clam closes its claw.
There's always snake oil potions.

A one-act set.
Not Sibelius's seeds growing organically
in the soil
and Pavlov, the dog, barking in the yard
to Sibelius's sad song.
But Spinoza's God, in other words, Nature
running the tumble dryer:
the little bird spinning your thoughts clean.

Killed.

There Were Two Words From The Frost

There were two words from the frost,
and one word from the ghost
to let me know that you still exist.
But you are gone, almost.
I mean in the frost melt,
listening to the voices of the old sea.

As potent, can I close my eyes now
and see the two words from the frost
and say three words to you
through my frozen tears, my winsome ghost?
I love you.

Uvalde Primary School, Texas

To use your colours and patterns to tell a lie,
mimicry, strange, strangeness
with figs alive with juice and wasps.
The maroon blew up a balloon
and let it go into the sky
through the figs, juice and wasps
to the grazing lands, with truths bent,
with the harmonies into a good clash
jingle jangly never to grow old and jaded.
Nineteen children, all under twelve, shot dead
by an eighteen-year-old with a rifle and a gun
at school, learning that love has no colour.

The Crooner

I could have been a crooner
with more natural talent than Frank Sinatra,
an episode in time.
My crooning could have been sublime,
but for you.
Even with delusions I could hold your hand
and curate the golden thread
that Grandma stitched in your hair,
to show me the promised land.

I could have been Ol' Blue Eyes,
when crooners could actually sing
in vermilion tones, with gravelly damask,
which I could have attached to your beauty
in Eliot's hyacinth bed.

Or as a Yank I met once said to me,
'Shakespeare sucks'. I was asked by another
Yank if I understood.
I replied 'Yes I do, the Yank sucks'
and sang the reply as a crooner
with the Ol' Blue Eyes.